HAIKU REVISITED

HAIKU REVISITED

Louis Cuneo

CELESTIAL ARTS
Millbrae, California

CELESTIAL ARTS
231 Adrian Road, Millbrae, California 94030

Originally published by Mother's Hen,
San Francisco, California

First printing: September 1975
Made in the United States of America

Library of Congress Cataloging in Publication Data

Cuneo, Louis.
      Haiku revisited.

      1. Haiku--History and criticism. I. Title.
PS3553.U467H3   1975   811'.5'4   74-25841
ISBN 0-89087-014-4

Basho quote on half title page is from R. H. Blyth,
Anthology of Modern Japanese Poetry. Rutland, Vt.:
Charles E. Tuttle, 1972.

A Haiku is not a poem, it is not literature; it is a hand beckoning, a door half open, a mirror wiped clean .... It is a silent language because it only beckons to a certain region, and does not explain why and where and how.

R. H. Blyth, *Haiku*, vol. 1, Eastern Culture. Tokyo: Hokuseido Press, 1949. Pp. 272-273.

ACKNOWLEDGMENTS

Marta N. Hoyos Cuneo for her art work and title; Dennis Koran, Edward Mycue and Peter Kastmiler for constructive and valid criticism; Barbara Maitles and Joe Ramos for their photography.

CONTENTS

Chapter One 10
    History of Haiku

Chapter Two 12
    Why Update Haiku?

Chapter Three 14
    Masoku Shiki

Chapter Four 17
    Twentieth Century Haiku Innovators

Chapter Five 26
    My Updating

Chapter Six 36
    Traditional Haiku

Chapter Seven 43
    Updated Haiku

Chapter Eight 71
    Long Haiku

Chapter Nine 93

Chapter Ten 94

7

To Kobayashi Issa (1762–1826)
for being very human and writing fine
Haiku.

Everything I touch
with tenderness, alas
pricks like a bramble.

Well! hello down there,
friend snail! When did you arrive
in such a hurry?

Haikus by Issa from *Haiku Harvest;* Mount Vernon,
N.Y.: Peter Pauper Press.

HAIKU REVISITED

CHAPTER ONE

CHINESE POETRY
Romance, nostalgia, world-weariness and evocations of glory which Haiku avoids. (Basho constantly read this for its spirit, not form.)

BUDDHISM
The foundation for simple directness and instantaneous perception.*

INDIAN BUDDHISM

WAKA
The use of Haiku words make it different from this poetry. The new vocabulary can be used instead of poetic diction to express. The form is 5-7-5-7-7.

CHINESE BUDDHISM

JAPANESE BUDDHISM

RENGA
Easier than waka and free and easy as Haiku. The form is 5-7-5, 7-7, 5-7-5, 7-7 for fifty or more verses by two or more people.

After R. H. Blyth, *Eastern Culture*, Volume 1. Tokyo: Hokuseido Press, 1949. *Author's additions to Blyth's chart.

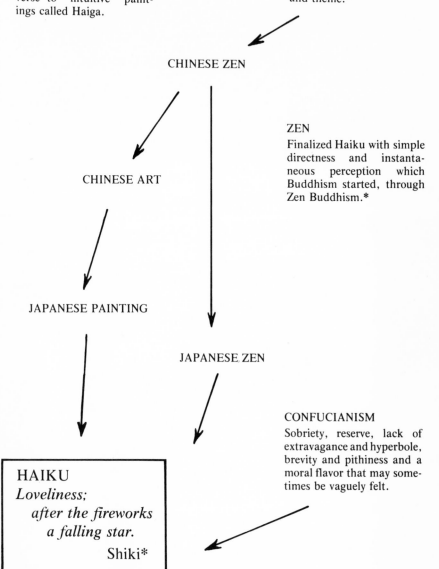

ORIENTAL ART
Haiku writers added their verse to "intuitive" paintings called Haiga.

TAOISM
Nature as the focal point and theme.*

CHINESE ZEN

ZEN
Finalized Haiku with simple directness and instantaneous perception which Buddhism started, through Zen Buddhism.*

CHINESE ART

JAPANESE PAINTING

JAPANESE ZEN

CONFUCIANISM
Sobriety, reserve, lack of extravagance and hyperbole, brevity and pithiness and a moral flavor that may sometimes be vaguely felt.

HAIKU
Loveliness;
*   after the fireworks*
*   a falling star.*
                Shiki*

CHAPTER TWO:
WHY UPDATE HAIKU?

Haiku was formed in the feudal period when Japan was controlled by the shoguns in the late 17th century A.D. by Matsuo Basho from the writing called Renga. It was a time of serfs, samurais, lords, and a completely agrarian economy.

In contrast, presently we are in a period of late industralization, as Japan is, and live with hundred-story buildings, jet power, urban culture, atom bombs, million-fold population and ever-increasing technology.

There are thirteen states of mind in traditional Haiku: selflessness, loneliness, grateful acceptance, wordlessness, non-intellectuality, contradiction, humor, freedom, non-morality, simplicity, materiality, love and courage. Further, they are all heavily defined by Zen and do not have the same meanings as we know in the Judeo-Christian culture and history.

12

A Japanese student here for only six months, attending San Francisco State College, told me that every time she sees the moon she feels about it as Basho did and that very few poets in Japan are writing Haiku now because they do not feel they can express themselves without copying one of the masters.

The influence of R. H. Blyth, James Hackett, Harold G. Henderson, Virginia K. Anderson, Gerald Robert Vizenor, *Haiku Highlights* magazine and other Western authorities promoting the writing of traditional Haiku would return us to 17th century Japan. They have made Haiku just a "cute Christmas gift" or a "pretty oriental novelty." They think they are bringing Haiku into the "limelight" or "advancing it." They are helping to destroy it by refusing to accept that THIS IS THE 20TH CENTURY AND THE WESTERN WORLD!

Even so, I commend Mr. Blyth and Mr. Henderson for letting me and others know what Haiku is in the traditional form. They have brought the orthodox form of Haiku to the Western world. Now it is up to us to make Haiku a live writing form! Let us start now, because the future is bright for self-expression, writing as a whole and Haiku!

CHAPTER THREE:
MASOKU SHIKI (1867–1902)

Masaoku Shiki started on the road of reform when he startled the Haiku world with his famous "Criticism of Basho" in 1893. Previously Master Basho's rule of the poetic form was unquestioned and languished in traditional beauty.

In another article, he selected as a model for his own school Buson, a conscious innovator and stylist despite his artificiality.

And so with a mind toward reform Shiki gave advice to beginners:

Be natural.

Don't bother about old rules of grammar and special points like spelling.

Read the old masters, remembering that in them you will find good and bad poems mixed.

Notice that commonplace Haiku is not direct, but artificially twisted out of place.

Write to please yourself. If your writing does not please you, how can you expect it to please anybody else?

14

Remember perspective. Large things are large but small things are also large if seen close up.

Delicacy should be studied, but it cannot be applied to human affairs in seventeen syllables. It can be applied to natural objects.

Haiku are not logical propositions, and no process of reasoning should show on the surface.

Keep the words tight, put in nothing useless.

Cut down as much as possible on adverbs, verbs and "postpositions."*

And more advice to his third class:

Read whatever you can, all worthwhile books on Haiku; think over their good and bad points.

Know all kinds of Haiku, but have your own style.

Gather new material directly; do not get it from old Haiku.

Know something about other literature also.

Know at least something about all art.*

---

*Harold G. Henderson, *An Introduction to Haiku*. New York: Doubleday & Co., Inc., 1958.

Looking at Haiku, now more than three centuries old, you must see and sample the past before you can realize the possibilities for today. What Master Shiki seriously attempted by expressing his views, is a historic record that should be studied, along with the other masters, with an innovator's eye.

In Chapter Five, "My Updating," I have corrected, kept or rejected his ideas until they have become my own advice for writing Haiku—today.

CHAPTER FOUR:
TWENTIETH CENTURY
HAIKU INNOVATORS

Mr. Blyth is the man who translated and interpreted Waka (a 31-syllable Japanese ode), Renku (linked verse of fifty or more verses by two or more people; form alternates between 5-7-5 and 7-7), No plays (drama in which movement represents stillness, and the stillness is not immobility but a perfect balance of opposed forces), Ikebana (flower arranging in which heaven, earth, and man are brought together in asymmetrical harmony), Cha no Yu (tea ceremony), Shinto (worship of deities of natural forces), and Haiku for the English speaking world. He gives a full understanding of all those forms within the traditional form.

R. H. Blyth is the teacher for traditional Haiku, and we in the Western world, who are interested in them, are his students. Now we have five Masters of Haiku to learn from: Basho, Buson, Issa, Shiki, and Blyth.

R. H. Blyth, *Haiku,* Vol. 1: Eastern Culture. Tokyo: Hokuseido Press.
———, *Haiku,* Vols. 2-3, *ibid.*
———, *History of Haiku,* Vols. 1-2, *ibid.*

HAROLD HENDERSON

Mr. Henderson does a complete job of attempting to fit Haiku into English language. His book, *Haiku in English,* explains to the beginners and interested persons the early steps in writing Haiku.

He comes from a Japanese base, not trying to find the true place for this form of writing in the Western experience. Still he has a book well worthwhile for beginners to consider seriously.

Harold G. Henderson, *Haiku in English*. Tokyo: Charles E. Tuttle Co.

EDITH MARCOME SHIFFERT and YUKI SAWA

Shiffert and Sawa's anthology has a section of the first collection of Japanese Haiku. It shows samples of Haiku by Japanese since the death of Master Shiki in 1902.

Some of the outstanding Haiku writers included in this book are Hekigodo Kawahigashi (1873-1937), Kyoshi Takahama (1874-1959), Seishi Yamaguchi (1901-), Takako Hashimoto (1899-1963), Kiyoko Tsuda (1920-), and Shigenobu Takayanagi (1923-), with brief biographical notes and samples of their work. Also, there is a fine selected bibliography about Haiku and other Japanese poetry.

Flashes of lightning
  in the intervals between
    the fireworks—now!
                    Hekigodo

A dewy tree trunk,
  without a sound a locust
    walking along.
                    Kyoshi

Up to the summer weeds
  wheels of a steam engine
    come and stop.
                    Seishi

All plucked off
  a chicken's feathers lying
    under a winter moon.
                    Takako

Greeness everywhere
  and inside it my own child's
    teeth starting to grow out.
                    Kusatao

*To be a mistress
is enough to tame me and
I cut a watermelon.*
                    Kiyoko

*Hear a war drum sound
and desolatedly
on autumn
      become a bruise mark.*
                    Shigenobu

Trs. Edith Marcome Shiffert and Yuki Sawa, *Anthology of Modern Japanese Poetry*. Tokyo: Charles E. Tuttle Co.

MAKOTA UEDA

Mr. Makota has compiled and written a concise history of Japanese Haiku since the 19th century entitled "Modern Japanese Haiku: New Poetry in an Antique Form," an essay. He has gone into great detail, but it is very easy to read; any interested person would enjoy reading it while being informed at the same time.

This essay adds to the list of modern Japanese writers of Haiku, besides the ones mentioned in *Anthology of Modern Japanese Poetry.* Saitō Sanki (1900-1962), Hino Sojo (1901-1956), and Akutagawa Ryunosuki (1892-1927).

The endless
falling snow, I wonder what
it is bringing to me.
Saitō

The wind of autumn:
a hair has begun to grow
on my mole.
Akutagawa

Spring evening's lamplight:
being a woman, she does not have
the Adam's apple.
Hino

Ed. William J. Higginson, *Haiku Magazine,* Double Issue 6 (1 and 2). Box 2702, Paterson, New Jersey 07509.

NOBUYUKI YUASA

Mr. Nobuyuki translates a field of Japanese literature, which is generally unknown to Western readers of creative writing; it is called *Haibun* (mixed form of Haiku and prose). He makes this form real and alive to the Western readers of Japanese traditional literature.

The Year of My Life is written by Master Issa whose writings are not as well known in the West as is Master Basho's Haibun, *The Narrow Road to the Deep North and Other Travel Sketches*, also translated by Mr. Nobuyuki.

In my estimation Master Issa is the greatest Master because he included humanism in Haiku, broke away from always writing about nature, included people and personal woes. Mr. Nobuyuki does great service to those who enjoy poetry by bringing Issa's work into English.

Issa, *The Year of My Life*, tr Nobuyuki Yuasa. Berkeley, Ca.: University of California.

JAMES HACKETT

Mr. Hackett is the first American Haiku writer being accepted by both the Japanese and American Haiku lovers. His work reflects his own style along with a knowledge of traditional Haiku. I really do not like his work because it seems derivative.

The Struggling ant
is suddenly unburdened
by his winged cargo.

James Hackett, *Haiku Poetry*, Vol. 3. Tokyo: Japan Publications Trading Co.

MICHAEL McCLINTOCK

When I find a Haiku writer, or a poet, or an artist, or any other creative person who brings me to some place special and indescribable, I don't intellectualize but let it be, flowing with *whatever* to *wherever*.

This is what Michael McClintock does for me.

Point Lobos

with the sea mist,
something of the night
it spent in the pines

washes the broomweed
vallied light, bent on
Mal Paso Mountain

the sea booms   immense distances

breakfast boils

the motion
her belly makes
stirring the pot

the small
of her back

& after the inevitable
poem we make

we watch

the gull's rilling flight & cry

the breakage,
the landward blowing of the sky

Louis Cuneo, ed., *Eastern Voices in America.* San Francisco: Mother's Hen, P. O. Box 99592, San Francisco, California 94109.

CAROL W. BRADLEY

Ms. Bradley writes in a warm, tender and personal sense, with the woman's touch, world outlook and feelings. She also follows the traditional rules with a strong knowledge of the subject.

She adds an element of sensuality and womanhood between her man and herself, nature and herself, motherhood and herself, and life and herself. She does have her own original style of freshness.

The first careful step
Native caution saves the day
When you're ten months old.

Carol W. Bradley, *Eastern Voices in America,* Anthology, San Francisco: Mother's Hen, Box 99592, San Francisco 94109.

RYAN ABE

Mr. Abe writes a narrative in Haiku. He is able to carry from the first to the last verse a story, but still keeping the spirit of Haiku. This is a most difficult goal to succeed in.

What Mr. Abe has done in his book, *Golden Sunrises,* is a breakthrough in concept for American Haiku. However, this work itself is somewhat repetitious; the narrative form has still to be advanced.

> *We had arisen*
> *shortly before dawn so we*
> *could greet the new day.*

Ryan Abe, *Golden Sunrises.* San Mateo, Ca.: Farris Press.

WILLIAM J. HIGGINSON

Mr. Higginson has compiled a book entitled *Haiku Checklist* which he describes as "An annotated bibliography of Haiku materials in English, will guide readers to translations, critical works, and books and magazines in English. A list of over 150 titles has been compiled with the aid of poets, editors and publishers on the four continents."

Ed. William J. Higginson, *Haiku Magazine,* Box 2602, Paterson, New Jersey 07509.

CHAPTER FIVE:
MY UPDATING

RULES

Without the first two below you don't write Haiku.

What is Haiku?

Mr. Basho gave us the only definition that explains Haiku: "Haiku is simply what is happening in this place, at this moment." I have found that this communicates more than anything written by myself, R. H. Blyth, James Hackett, or Harold Henderson.

Zen

In my updating, the only part of Zen thinking that should be kept is: "Your *ordinary mind and simplicity—that is the Way of Zen.*" The rest should be disregarded.

ADVICE

Read the Masters. You should read Basho for the spirit, Buson for form, Issa for humanism, Shiki for the spirit of reform and Blyth for English translation and interpretation. Please don't put them on golden thrones, but look at them as everyday people who achieved The Way with failure and successes.

Spirit Not Form

Haiku is spirit, not form. It's seeing a leaf falling without any thought; feeling love but unable to have it; smelling garbage in the slum and getting angry; eating too much pizza at one sitting and you can't get up; thinking how great it was at a friend's place and you had to go; a conflict between you and the neighbor across the hall over the noise; or waiting for happiness but sadness stays.

Book Suggestions for Orthodox or Traditional Haiku

See chapter four.

Kenneth Yasuda, *Japanese Haiku.* Mount Vernon, N.Y.: Peter Pauper Press.

Harold G. Henderson, *An Introduction to Haiku.* Garden City, N.J.: Doubleday, 1958.

Kenneth Yasuda, *Japanese Haiku: Its Essential Nature, History and possibilities in English.* Tokyo: Charles E. Tuttle Co.

Kobayashi Issa, *The Autumn Wind.* N.Y.: Paragon.

Matsuo Basho, tr. Nobuyuki Yuasa, *Narrow Road to the Deep North and Other Travel Sketches.* Baltimore: Penguin.

Upasaka Shiki, tr. Harold J. Isaacson, *Peonies Kana.* N.Y.: Theatre Arts.

Asataro Miyamori, ed., *Anthology of Haiku, Ancient and Modern.* Westport, Conn.: Greenwood Press.

Any book on Haiku from anyone and WRITE YOUR OWN ESSAY ABOUT YOUR OWN STYLE AND PUBLISH IT!

Traditional Haiku

To express yourself right away before learning the Japanese style is harmful because you won't have any background in Haiku and your work probably will be prose or poetry in Haiku form, and Haiku is neither.

> *In this vacant lot*
> *a spider builds*
> *his web from a rock.*

5-7-5 Form

First work with this without breaking it. This is only the beginning of the discipline needed to find *The Way.* After you feel (not know) you have gained *The Way,* you will flow into any amount of syllables within two or three lines as you feel appropriate. But as soon as you start to say too much, phony I-ism or too deep, you should return to 5-7-5 until you clean your mind out again.

> *One whole day went by*
> *I haven't seen you at all. . .*
> *I missed you so much!*

Simplicity

Never be complicated! Just describe what is, was or will be with a quick thought (not deep) or action or feeling. GIVE A SIMPLE STATEMENT AND AVOID ALL USELESS AND EXTRA WORDS!

> *You're leaving now*
> *For your own life. . .*
> *While I'm staring*
> *At the night*
> *Through the kitchen window.*

> *You're leaving now*
> *while I'm staring*
> *through kitchen window.*

Everyday Language and Subjects

Use everyday language and subjects, as actions, experiences, speech and words. Basho planned Haiku from the start to be "Every Man's Writing," not the intellectual's or literary genius'. I wholly agree with this as one of the basic foundations of my updating Haiku.

> *Smiling people in this room. . .*
> *stop it*
> *before I scream!*

Nothingness

The subject is impossible to write down because it is not intellectual or solid, but a vague live feeling. After you have achieved *The Way,* it will be plain as the sunshine and show in your life and Haiku. This Haiku is the only way I have found to explain this.

*Cockroach crossing the street
while two cars are coming.*

Not Poetry or Prose

Haiku does not have poetic rhythm or any other characteristic of poetry or prose. It has the NATURAL FLOW OF LIFE, not preconceived style. It is in a class of its own in the world of literature throughout history. Only some American Indian poetry comes close, especially from eastern woodland tribes as in *Heaps of Clouds:* Great heaps/of clouds/in the direction I am looking.*

American Indian Poetry, edited by George W. Cronyn, Ballantine Books, page 14.

The day at work was so pressing and
  difficult.
When I came home at six,
We had a fight over some petty subject
As two little kids arguing over a toy.
I went to my desk to write.
I heard the radio playing some loud music.
It made me nervous.
I got up to turn it off. . .
Silence is settling my mind, heart and
  body.

The music from the radio
  making me very nervous. . .
    my being longs for silence.

Titles

Titles should not be included because the Haiku
must tell what you expressed within "it."

Description

Make it concise, mundane and real. Do not use
symbolism, abstractions, poetic terms or adjectives
and adverbs like whispering grass, enchanted heart
or rarely-ever-known.

Cry. . . cry!
  broken hearted man. . .
    let the sorrow come out!

Protest and Struggle

Men and women have protested and struggled against war, poverty, all kinds of oppression, no jobs, lack of crops, and bad governments from the earliest recorded history. Haiku must, also, reflect this progressive force as poetry and other art forms have.

> *Great battle scene:*
> *Soldiers in mortal combat*
> *while the generals worry.*

Indirect or Direct Technique

In traditional Haiku, the subtle way of telling is the rule, except in most of Issa's work. But in my updating, ideas or feelings can be expressed either way.

> *Through the dirty window*
> *the sun. . .*
> *brightens the room*

> *Dirty kitchen,*
> *you need me*
> *to clean you up.*

Humor

Please don't forget or omit humor, it is part of life just as sadness, self-fullness, nothingness, and the rest. Only one thing is advised: Don't get clever or cute. Keep it earthbound.

> *Working on summer job*
> *she smokes a cigarette*
> *with her mother.*

Tense

It could be in the past tense, present or future because we, as human beings, live in all of these. I advise you to stay in "Now" because you might otherwise destroy the pure moment.

> *Eighty-three dollar*
> *phone bill came. . .*
> *I nearly fainted.*

> *Beach full of people*
> *swimming or sunbathing. . .*
> *deep blue sky!*

> *New York,*
> *in eight months. . . I'll*
> *see your beauty and ugliness!*

Natural I-ism

In the orthodox form, *I* is omitted. But in my updating, it is an important part because *I* happens to *be*, like it or not. Watch out for phony I-isms or too many! Remember there is a big wide world of subjects out there!

> *Tonight I'm*
> *wearing all blue*
> *to meet my mood.*

Retouching or Rewriting

I would advise not to rewrite *unless* it is done WITHIN the exact moment without any intellectual thought, because you will not permit *cleaning* of your mind and kill the *moment's life* and *uniqueness*. If you write and fail, you should accept and wait until it returns again.

Intellectualism

It should be mundane or very, very light, not any deep philosophical statement, implied or inferred. The work might do that accidentally, but let it happen and do not try.

> *Walking in the night alone*
> *seeing the bright moon. . .*
> *recalling Basho's walking trip.*

Long Haiku

This is a whole experience that is put together from individually written Haiku on the same subject without any time period. If the first Haiku does not state the place, situation, or theme, add a title to make the work clearer for the reader. Let the experience give you the beginning, middle and end. Also, never try to arrange them because you might (almost for sure) kill the spirit of Haiku and turn it into a prose or poetry in two or three line segments.

I gave you a big worm,
  dear small tree,
    to keep you company and healthy.

I washed each leaf
  of yours. . .
    now you can breathe better.

Hey! you have
  eight new tiny leaves
    since yesterday.

Christmas eve
  I'm putting the lights
    and many colored bulbs. . . on you.

CHAPTER SIX:
TRADITIONAL HAIKU

Sound of birds talking
in dense park. . .
nowhere to be seen.

* * *

Even the kitten rests
after he has eaten,
as we do.

* * *

Iced trees by mountain road
with trucks traveling
in snowstorm.

Flow of the stream
  passing through forest. . .
    makes sweet music.
      *   *   *

After leaving
  a small coastal beach. . .
    missing the sea mist.
      *   *   *

Old brick pathway
  wild grasses growing between bricks...
    slowly covering.

That wooden fence by
  dirt road near the ocean...
    remembering it clearly.

The willow tree's branches
twisting, flying in all directions...
four a.m.

*Through the dirty window
the sun
brightens the room.*

Next to old tree...
single blade of grass flapping
in autumn dusk.

* * *

Hear the ocean crashing
while seagulls search...
early morning.

* * *

Through the hardened soil
flowers are blooming...
weak stems.

Hey, laughing youths,
mocking an old man . . . you will
be old soon enough.

       *   *   *

Trunk of things from
last home . . . I always
forget to send for it.

       *   *   *

Old tom walks
on low wall by
small Japanese tea garden.

43

Right now!
all of me has The Way. . .
I feel free!

*   *   *

Rain rushes toward
the street. . .
miniature flood!

*   *   *

Empty bag of homemade cookies
lying in ash tray. . .
retasting each bite . . . slowly.

*   *   *

Friendly Stranger, my dead cat,
you are still deep in my heart. . .
after a year.

I called you long distance. . .
how I have changed from
when we saw each other everyday!

* * *

Performer,
preparing to do your set. . .
please make me happy!

* * *

The street lamps
reflect across the pond
through Greek pillars.

* * *

She's getting dressed
to go out . . .
singing while putting on makeup.

Two wrestlers in Olympics,
the top one is trying
to turn over the other.

* * *

Damn!
awaking in donut shop. . .
without today's newspaper!

* * *

Santa Cruz,
it's so hard to leave
you . . . each time.

* * *

Hulk, your eyes are fire . . .
can anybody save you
from your personal hell?

Throwing balls at bottles . . .
he wins and
tosses his coat at girlfriend.

      *   *   *

Vacant neighborhood center
with dusty windows . . .
Join the new majority,' pleaded Nixon.

      *   *   *

Shit!
I'm getting fatty all over
and showing . . . tiny double chin.

      *   *   *

In this ash tray . . .
there are four cigarette butts
and five burnt matches.

Clear light bulb smashed
on floor during the day . . .
the Milky Way!

*   *   *

He threatens to take away
my job promotion . . .
every damn day.

*   *   *

Yes, I hear your voice . . .
you are destroying
my sleepy-morning bliss.

*   *   *

Part of porno movie . . .
young girl getting
Greeked and . . . liking it.

I read your letter . . .
remembering your words:
I miss our long talks together.

* * *

Barefoot Doctor,
you act everyday
while I'm just talking.

* * *

Teenager with parents together,
please tell me how
it feels growing up?

* * *

Two Mayan headdresses
with feathers in corner . . .
covered by plastic bag.

Halloween night
  not one child came trick-or-treat . . .
    what's happening?

        * * *

You have returned . . .
  I can't take
    my eyes off you!

        * * *

Little girl stands in front
  of the ladies' room . . .
    door open.

        * * *

She stares at wall
  holding glass of beer . . .
    not looking around.

Looking at apartment . . .
  walls creaking and dirty
    for one-hundred fifty per month.

* * *

The sun isn't out
  and wind blows hard . . .
    sidewalk deserted.

* * *

Hearing the bath water running . . .
  I see kitchen grease and dirt
    flow down the drain.

* * *

You won't destroy
  my spirit of defiance and integrity . . .
    boss!

Little house being torn down . . .
making more room
for parking lot.

Rain falling on
window . . . creating
new dimension of the world.

* * *

Tomorrow get out of
my mind . . . I'll meet
you when the sun rises!

* * *

Dreaming*
Standing on an
interstate highway with my
thumb out . . . at daybreak.

* * *

Hearing an old Dylan song . . .
reliving a large part
of my early life.

*Everything in life has an exception to the rule. This is one.

Harsh wind . . . please stop
kicking us out
of this peaceful park.

* * *

Discussing war tactics
over drinks . . . ignoring
the misery and death.

* * *

Don't worry, typewriter,
you will get well . . .
Cuneo is here!

* * *

Mother! Mother!
is it true:
you will die someday?

Here I come
   as you asked me to.

      *   *   *

A white wall
   with many spots of food
      and cracks.

      *   *   *

The tide takes
   river towards the ocean . . .
      also, carrying wet paper.

      *   *   *

After the softball game
   both teams drink . . .
      replaying each hit.

She licks the cream
off the glass . . .
full of cappucino.

* * *

House of the Rising Sun
is playing on radio . . .
oh, New Orleans, you are dying!

* * *

Lovers! be kind to each other . . .
because the world outside
is rarely gentle and understanding.

* * *

As she sits,
I imagine her
firm and exciting body . . . nude.

*Multiplying and dividing fractions
  for one hour . . .
    my head aches!*

        *   *   *

*Shit!
  I can't write
    until I go to the bathroom.*

        *   *   *

*Secondhand wicker chair
  with broken seat . . .
    full of two peoples' clothes.*

        *   *   *

*So you complain about the rape
  of American Imperialism in South America . . .
    let's destroy it now!*

*All day was cold
and rainy . . . I didn't go out
once.*

*   *   *

*He tells us that
he's a poet before
we know his name.*

*   *   *

*Finished with the toilet . . .
realizing that no more
toilet paper is in house.*

*   *   *

*Happy New Year's Eve,
Cuneo . . . again you will
be working in the kitchen!*

*Woman! you have
such exciting legs . . . I can't
take my eyes from them.*

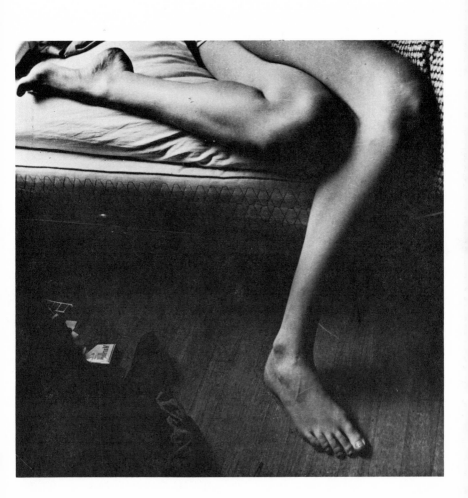

We walked across town
  in chilly night air . . . how time
  passed with our talking.

          *   *   *

African head broken . . .
  artist putting it together
  with careful and loving care.

          *   *   *

Driftwood slowly
  touching the shore
  by little bay waves.

          *   *   *

Your phone call
  and this bleak morning . . .
  why did I wake up!

Group of children playing
near decaying houses
with dog shit . . . all around.

*   *   *

Wine bottle and can
of beans empty in
pile of bus transfers.

*   *   *

Once we talked . . .
now we don't see
each other in the same room.

*   *   *

Child returns from dentist . . .
her father hugs her
and tells something in Chinese.

"If it weren't for
a few friends like you . . .
I wouldn't make it." *

* * *

Thank you, my friend,
letting me read
your great poems.

* * *

He finished urinating . . .
shakes his penis
and puts it in.

* * *

Such pleasure to see . . .
breasts bouncing
in a light blouse.

---

*Text by Bruce Chaiet, arranged by the author.

Hell . . .
  I can't function
    without damn cigarettes!

      * * *

The weight lifter holds
  497 pounds on his shoulders . . .
    waiting for the signal.

      * * *

Woman abiding
  a red light . . .
    very chilly wind.

      * * *

I don't have any place
  where my heart feels
    this is my home.

Thank you, big-eyed child,
  for chasing the self-pity from me . . .
    by saying bye-bye.

Peace rumors are flying
around the world . . . while
mankind waits and dies.

*   *   *

This Japanese tea garden
dirty and dying flowers
in back of Japanese restaurant.

*   *   *

She had to become
a human guinea pig . . .
so she would have bus fare.

*   *   *

"You two have the
green thumb," she told us . . .
the plant is dead.

I am getting sick, lobsters!
I must pick one of you
for the cook's knife.

*   *   *

The fog covered
the city all morning
until the afternoon.

*   *   *

The food stamp office . . .
mother holds her infant
with one package of stamps.

*   *   *

The sound of dishes
being put through machine by
hardworking dishwasher!

Reading book on history
  of American labor strikes . . . each page
  makes me cry.

    *   *   *

It's your birthday!
  I'm so happy
    being here for it!

Long Haiku No. 2

Again, riding on Greyhound bus . . .
  seeing the open country
    fly by.

A young mother
  puts a fur coat
    on her child.

Some rebellious water
  flows
    into a tiny cove.

In VW bus
  young boy picks his head up
    from sleeping bag.

71

"Don't worry.
  Just go to city hall
    and ask for information."

Green hills
  standing next to
    the rolling river.

The motor makes
  most irritating sound
    while we are all silent.

As she passes . . .
  she inspects each window
    with hard stare.

The bus turns . . .
  we hear the wheels rub
    against something.

Santa Cruz!
  Soon I'll smell
    your ocean air!

Finding paper about my job
  while strolling along beach . . .
    I throw it away.

Form of wave rushes
  forward over dried sand
    and seaweed and footprints.

Mother building sandcastle
  with her son . . .
    toy shovel in hand.

Make room for the sea gulls!
  it's their home . . .
    we are just their guests!

Bunch of seaweed loose
  is being carried back to sea
    by the undertow.

She studying some song
  on guitar . . .
    her children playing away.

The sound of waves
  crashing against
    the jutting rocks!

Couple walking . . .
  wearing loud bathing suits
    along bleached pathway.

The shape-cliffed valley
  with many large redwoods . . .
    what a view!

The beach long gone . . .
  now I'm in the world
    of cement and buildings.

Indian corn and small pumpkin
  lying on apartment floor . . .
    in the dark.

Choir . . . sing your heart out!
  make my mouth shout:
    Hallelujah! Hallelujah!

Long Haiku No. 3

Water bugs,
  I see you are enjoying the game
    of tag.

Be careful!
  the birds are looking
    at you.

There you go
  for a ride
    down those tiny rapids.

The bird slopes down . . .
  lands with water bug
    in mouth.

Long Haiku No. 4

Looking out the window
  with my kitten
    during the night.

Everything is silent
  and apartments' light on . . .
    few passing cars.

At eleven p.m. . . . .
  fire engine after fire engine
    rushes by.

Outside of bar
  few young people passing . . .
    cigarette in the shadows.

Sidewalk being enlarged . . .
  now pit
    for trash and dog shit.

Tonight there's block party
  with rainbow-colored lights
    and many people.

Woman carrying white poodle,
  talking to him . . .
    one a. m.

Faint sounds of singer
  from across the way . . .
    cable car making noise.

It's Friday night . . .
  many motors
    being heard.

There they go!
  arm and arm down the street . . .
    laughing.

Long Haiku No. 5

Eight a.m. before work
I sit in dining room . . .
looking out through plate glass.

Medium-sized freighter leaving
port at early morning . . .
covered in dense fog.

Fisherman getting off boat
with his catch and gear . . .
not single tourist watching.

American flag all wet
  trying to wave . . .
    middle of heavy rainstorm.

Workman holding box of fish
  while superior speaks . . .
    in front of fish company.

Lone person walking on beach
  during dark cloudy morning . . .
    far from where I'm sitting.

At two a.m.
  taxicab riding on street
  and no tourists.

Blinking lights on-off . . .
  many single lights
    flickering behind it.

Cats starting to
come on roofs
of all the fish companies.

Heavy wind blows . . .
moving branches of tree
next to street lamp.

Across the bay
the hills light
like thousands of candles.

Noise of garbage truck
driving down the street . . .
breaking the silence.

In empty parking lot . . .
man closing the booth
with his coat on.

Long Haiku No. 6

Dear little kitten,
  you are safe from the street . . .
    still you cry.

Walking past her
  as she eats chicken . . .
    she growls at me.

Please . . .
  stop playing
    with the pen as I am writing!

Mechanical dog wags
  its tail . . .
    she's preparing to attack.

I'm picking fleas
  from her head . . .
    she has her ears down.

Writing a Haiku . . .
  she's demanding attention . . .
    I stop to pick her up.

She comes on bed . . .
  I say, "No, Pochita Linda" in
    gentle voice . . . she turns around.

Archie the tom
  walks in . . .
    she chases him out.

Hey!
  I'm not the sparring partner
    for your newly found claws.

Six in the morning,
  she climbs over our bodies . . .
    sleeps on the pillow.

Live your own life!
get used to being a cat . . .
not a dog!

"Pochita Linda has broken
  my African head piece . . .
    but I can fix it."

Why do you give me
  the dirty stare . . .
    when I'm cleaning your eyes?

Why are you
  chasing
    your own shadow?

OK! have patience
  I am changing your box . . .
    right now!

Another tom and Pochita eyeing
  each other . . . she smells
    him . . . tom strikes.

So she waits
  at the door
    meows, meows all day.

She came home from
    first night of lovemaking . . .
        she is cleaning herself.

"Pochita Linda. Linda Pochita,"
    I say lovingly . . . she
        comes with quiet meow.

She sits in open
    window . . . watching the
        rain drops hit.

Hey! why do you
    attack my feet
        when I don't move them?

Making love at midnight . . .
    local tom calls
        for her.

For the last two days
    she has been gone . . .
        we are very worried!

"Pochita Linda . . ."
 she comes running and I
 carry her home.

Thank you, Mrs. Jones,
 for calling us . . .
  this Haiku is for you.

Freezing night . . .
 she's cleaning herself
 between her legs.

Tom calls over and over . . .
 she lays there
  without moving her head.

"Pochita, we are moving
 tomorrow. Don't worry
 about anything."

My wife takes her
 out of traveling case . . .
  she hides behind cartons.

As we unpack . . .
  she checks out her new home.

Every room we go,
  she follows . . . but
    sits or lays by herself.

"When are you going
  to have your kittens?
    We are waiting."

I come home . . .
  she meows
    only once.

"She will have her
  kittens on the bed."
    "I hope not."

I open the door . . .
  she rushes out but
    returns quickly by herself.

*"Pochita, please have your
    babies when I'm here."*

*As she sleeps
    kicking from her stomach*

*I wake . . .
    she's going through labor
    one inch from my leg.*

*She turns to me
    with passive-defenseless expression . . .
    meows softly.*

Long Haiku No. 7

Cement house in ruins
  with half under soil . . .
    next to seacoast.

We are reading
  the graffiti on walls . . .
    laughing.

Beer cans
  among
    growth and broken glass.

My friend with hands
  around rusted iron bars saying,
    "I hate jails."

On dirty wall entrance . . .
  the painted word:
    women.

"What will you do
  about finding a job?
    "I don't know."

Tiny stream flows
  to sea with big dead tree
    over . . . roar of the surf.

When the morning comes . . .
  you will be gone,
    again.

You are driving
  down the street . . .
    I am missing you already!

CHAPTER NINE

Write your own Haiku

CHAPTER TEN:

Postcript

*Basho, would you approve
of what I'm doing
with your Haiku?*

celestial arts

LOVE IS MY REASON

WALTER RINDER
105-1   Paper $4.95

WILL YOU SHARE WITH ME?

WALTER RINDER
072-1   Paper $4.95

THIS OF JOY

JOY SIMMONS
024-1   Paper $3.95

OF A POET

BILL HARGER
30-8   Paper $2.95

THE WAYFARER

ROY PURCELL
07-1   Paper $4.95

VISIONS OF YOU

GEORGE BETTS
07-3   Paper $3.95

WILL I THINK OF YOU?

LEONARD NIMOY
70-7   Paper $3.95

LOVE IS AN ATTITUDE

03-0   Paper $3.95